THE NARROW CABINET

A Zombie Chronicle

ESSENTIAL POETS SERIES 293

**Canada Council
for the Arts**

**Conseil des Arts
du Canada**

**ONTARIO ARTS COUNCIL
CONSEIL DES ARTS DE L'ONTARIO**

Canadä

Guernica Editions Inc. acknowledges the support of the Canada Council
for the Arts and the Ontario Arts Council. The Ontario Arts Council
is an agency of the Government of Ontario.

We acknowledge the financial support of the Government of Canada.

ASA BOXER

THE NARROW CABINET

A Zombie Chronicle

GUERNICA EDITIONS

TORONTO – CHICAGO – BUFFALO – LANCASTER (U.K.)

2022

Guernica Founder: Antonio D'Alfonso

Michael Mirolla, editor
Cover and Interior Design: Errol F. Richardson
Guernica Editions Inc.
287 Templemead Drive, Hamilton (ON), Canada L8W 2W4
2250 Military Road, Tonawanda, N.Y. 14150-6000 U.S.A.
www.guernicaeditions.com

Distributors:
Independent Publishers Group (IPG)
600 North Pulaski Road, Chicago IL 60624
University of Toronto Press Distribution (UTP)
5201 Dufferin Street, Toronto (ON), Canada M3H 5T8
Gazelle Book Services
White Cross Mills, High Town, Lancaster LA1 4XS U.K.

First edition.
Printed in Canada.

Legal Deposit – First Quarter
Library of Congress Catalog Card Number: 2021949430
Library and Archives Canada Cataloguing in Publication
Title: The narrow cabinet / Asa Boxer.
Names: Boxer, Asa, author.
Series: Essential prose series ; 293.
Description: Series statement: Essential prose series ; 293 | Poems.
Identifiers: Canadiana 20210358793 | ISBN 9781771837170 (softcover)
Classification: LCC PS8603.O9767 N37 2022 | DDC C811/.6—dc23

Contents

2. Sinkhole

3. Zombie Apocalypse

Dedicated to the Shechinah
without whose influence there would be no poetry

THE OLD DISPENSATION

The Toolmaker

The hands that built the house I come from
murdered two men and fled and fled again
over land and sea and ocean, from Old Europe
deep into the Laurentian Mountains.

With those brutal hands, great granddad
cobbled a plane, cut its blade from a steel file,
turned out mallets, bowls and plates
from trees he'd felled to clear his ground.

He fashioned wooden clamps and vises
with wooden bolts he'd lathed with threads
on a lathe he'd built with those vital hands
from makeshift and scraps.

He was a toolmaker, a man who plans
the syntax of our labours, and with each new
tool, he'd rout, mitre, dowel, jig or dado
a further nuance in the service of beauty.

His muscles mastered each tool
and each tool in turn refigured the body:
a massive, castiron shoulder, a wrist
as round and knobbed as a steel faucet;

the tool determines where one twists
and tightens the rippled rigging of the back;
when to grind the femur's pestle
in the mortar of the knee, and heave;

and when to ply a giant elbow,
where employ the hip, when to stoop
and when bend in the ceremonies
of sawdust and joinery.

A copper handed, iron footed archetype,
he authored seven shivering children,
and, Biblically, thickened the plot amongst them
with rivalries unsettling generations.

In rage and jealousy, a near Olympian,
with him began the scurrilous fabliau
of the Canadian Boxer clan
now dwindling from the world.

His sons and grandsons built cottages,
but none thereafter knew the craft
of making tools. None were equal to the hands
that built the house they came from.

Iron Crow

With one sharp foot and one sharp squawk,
he wedged himself into wood and rock,
wrecking house and hearth,
prying the outlying geology apart.

Dusted in glistening carbon,
the iron crow was hatched
in the smoke and flash
of his maker's pneumatic hands.

And with his cloven beak, he plucked
nails that spangled our homes like stars,
and deaf to their steel screams,
he pulled them up like worms.

The Jimmy, we called him.
Or on account of his gooseneck,
Devil's Crook. He prised door from frame,
popped window locks.

He threatened all the marry-work.
Not a screw was safe. And in a glimmer,
he'd snaked into our brains.
And by abstraction there became

a question mark—a tool for mental prying.
First, he sundered man from woman;
then, building on this method, he sought
the cleft and chink in every item of perception.

And in the mind, his claw became
the casuist's scalpel. The heart's order
that he'd stripped and wrecked on earth,
he found and overturned again within.

Once he'd found his perch, it was all one could do
to conk the iron bird like a tuning fork,
attend to the dreadful note and adjust
one's instruments to his discord.

Tending the Tree of Knowledge

A true and pious index finger juices guilt and shame
from these orbs, swinging in God's hothouse.

Irreconcilable how they emerge from delicate petals,
these tiny sparks swelling slowly into sweet fireballs,

and how the blossoms cupping them arise in the first place
quietly as a rash of whispered accusations.

Perhaps less incongruous, what lusty colour imbues
and what odour of anticipation attends

the trumpeting of so savage a call
among the jagged leaves and the stark twigs.

The Invention of Money

It began as a sign, a stand-in for the real thing,
an intention to reward labour with roof and food;
it was a promise of cheese and chickens, bolts
of cloth, flour and honey—a promise, nothing more.

And so it was, until that fateful day
when Angus gave Stephen's note away
and Jack came calling on Stephen,
which, frankly, did not go well,

for Stephen had given that note to Angus
on account of a milk goat he now fed ...
none of which, by his reckoning,
had anything to do with Jack.

Jack, however, was a clever man,
especially gifted when it came to holding
others responsible for his errors,
and so it seemed obvious to him

how little it mattered whether the deal
was struck with Angus or Martin
(or even with Helga!). It was all the same.
If you asked Stephen, though, he was adamant:

he'd never trade with the likes of Jack,
and so his promise did not extend to him.
So Jack asked who he would deal with,
and Stephen replied, *Almost anyone.*

So Jack did the only sensible thing
and took his note elsewhere, and let
Amos trade the bill in his stead, though not
before Amos had given him some hens.

Soon enough everyone was doing it;
and began shifting these promises
until they were no longer affairs of the hands
but something else entirely: for instance,

it is uncertain whether Stephen ever
had to fulfil his promise. Likely his note
wound up travelling so far from him,
he never did see it again. It had become

a new creature, emerged straight out
of the imagination, with its own beak, its own
feathers and talons, entrancing folk. Behold,
the fanciful, flighty career of this amazing brain fowl.

Now here's where the story gets weird.
This peacock of the mind gets loose, you see;
it gets into the world and one day, Jack
catches the bird. Immediately it explodes,

leaving a cloud of smoke and a hot, heavy
mass of coal in its place. And what does Jack do?
Gets spooked and runs. Then Stephen, hearing
of the affair, hunts it, cracks it, and strikes gold.

Old School

I wouldn't say *regret* but a boring cousin of regret,
like *disappointed*. Truly? It's like Dad's tale
about growing up amidst stories of Chikevitch:
the Rasputin of La Macaza, Quebec who'd gallop
through town standing on two horses like a drunken
Cossack on a pogrom, firing two revolvers at God;
and how twenty years later, Dad met the aged version,
and how he was short as a nineteenth century door
—no way those legs could ever have spanned two horses,
(two donkeys? perhaps). It's that brand of psychic loss:
disillusion and nihilism lurk there at the crux.
Then, one day, Chikevitch says; he says, "That cancer
isn't going to kill me; I'm going to kill it first." So
he rigs a rifle to a tree, ties a knot around the trigger
and faces the barrel. And that was his final burlesque:
Chikevitch Pries the Scythe from the Fist of Death.

Chuck Fipke

I approach the world as I would face a tribe
of cannibals clad in armour and warpaint:
with courage enough and a readiness to trade
my shirt, trade my pants for dear life
and stand buck naked in the back-bush
of New Guinea, the Amazon and Africa,
exposed to every death, knocking at the door
of the earth as if to say, *Here I am. Infest me:*
let your parasites crawl under my skin
and feast awhile, for I belong to the earth.
Thus I cast myself into her deepest jungles
seeking her secrets in silt and stone: where
her copper veins, where the laces of silver
and gold, in which pipes her diamonds lie.
Either she will tolerate my prying, my staking
claims, or she'll absorb and knead me
back into herself; but I'll be damned if I peter
and play it safe—subsist to die of nothing.

Frank Cole

I crossed the Sahara on foot and camel-back.
No kind of living could knock the sand out of me after.
I put civilisation behind me, spent ten years with that year,
cutting and splicing, viewing and reviewing the miles
of footage I'd snatched from that country of death.
I should have died there. It is there I was forged.
Seven camels dropped, but I, despite all the signs, survived.
Having endured Hades, no greater crossing remains.
The eye of the Sahara still grips me in its blue whorl.
Though such beauty will not abide us long,
yet I will have her, and she, with her fire, will cure me
the way she cured this ancient sea.

The Great Wallenda

After Michael Harris

I keep revisiting this tightrope walk
across a gaping chasm. The tense cable
is familiar: stretched thin as hope.
I amble out and hang with God.
You might think I've taken these
thousand careful steps a thousand times before,
and like a seasoned driver, I can glide along
eating and talking on the phone.
Perhaps you surmise it's all practice:
maybe the secret's to imagine
you're just a few safe feet above ground.
But I assure you, I indulge no illusion.
Do you really think I'd turn my mind
to football at such a sublime, ecstatic
moment in the evolutionary march?
Death is not a lady I aim to please.
Why would I walk this narrow path
if not for the crashing rush, the gnashing,
slavering jaws of Niagara Falls, if not
to peer down the throat of Grand Canyon?
The trick's to take in the beauty,
to throb with the thrill but to take it in stride,
to let it ride over you, around you,
but never through you like a chill.
Be alert and beware your instincts.
Your every reflex works against you
when you're teetering at the verge of the void.
I aim to overcome the vertiginous awe,
aware that should my ear twitch too curiously

toward some unexpected sound, or should
a peripheral shadow cause my eye
to jitter and that jitter trip a quake, why,
I should surely pivot and fall.
Until then, I must mind each step.
Where I stand is too profound
to pretend I'm somewhere else.

Jacques Mayol

I plunged as deep into myself
as into the swaying sea
and freed the dolphin sleeping
there under chains of memory.
But I sensed I was mere fathoms
away from some lordlier creature
that kept the key to endless breath.
I longed to possess that gift,
enough to feel inklings
of metamorphosis
tingle through my limbs;
not that any webbing
ever grew between my toes,
but tired of relentless gravity,
fed up with the terrestrial plod,
I dreamt such changes.
I felt I had my finger
on an evolutionary trigger,
that one day I'd inhale and have
all I'd ever need of this world.

The Old Time-Cabinet

I bought the whole harmless façade:
the grandfatherly mien, shoulders hunched,
arthritic hinges, an immobile front
and that quaint, transparent pane to the guts.
Then it happened, going out for milk
and the morning paper, I returned to find
virtue, beauty, love—had all been swept
into that narrow cabinet. (Well, at least
that's how it felt.) Now at forty, the world
I was raised for is past. Happily, where I've been,
my heart has led; all I know, my heart has said.
But the tree-of-life Time trims with progeny,
Time has not trimmed for me. Clearer now
where my desire and my portion part.
The moonish circle of the clockface lies
about what grave work goes on inside:
the weights that drive the revolution
are ticking down, but so gradually,
you don't get the sense of falling
and unravelling that's really going on.

The Mountain

After A.M. Klein

Where now a wide concrete staircase blisters
upon the western lip of Fletcher's Field
was once the mouth to a piss-foul, piss-rotten
walking tunnel—dim place of switchblades and needles—
dread passage of grim graffiti and shards of glass

gleaming the way to a wilderness of perverts
and child-snatchers, crouching in the darkness
among the trees. A boy who went exploring
might lose his way—his likeness to be found
some weeks later haunting a carton of milk.

Not until my heart was hammered on the anvil
of my father's deathbed and annealed in the furnace
of hot-tempered adolescence, did I,
randy and angry, find the balls to mount her slopes.
Summer nights leading up to the last decade

of the millennium, I'd follow a pheromone trail
up Murray Hill to the clock-tower, and under
the glowing full moon of its clockface, past curfew,
I, hot under the collar and playing it cool,
met dangerous girls, who—with the fragrance

flung from a flourish of their hair—could drive
boys to handspringing, beer-guzzling, smoking, cursing.
For a dénouement, filing west along Westmount Avenue,
laughing and hollering, high on hormone,

we'd cross the powerful lamps at the foot
of a yellow-brick convent—our shadows projected
some forty feet up the wall—what gargantuan forms
we could raise upon the stark immovables
of this staunch, Catholic mountain.

Old Victorian Walk-Up

The stairwell door is a misfit,
leaning roughly in a tilted frame.
A precarious kiss of brass tongue
and brass lip barely holds
these two together. And still
you must jiggle, spin and jostle
an absurdly loose knob to tease
the tongue back in, and again
to release it and close the door.
There's no way in or out
without this fuss. Always the door
and his mate stammering,
being either rattled in union,
or tricked apart with a clamour.
So steep is the staircase, it is
nearly a ladder. It seems a trial
meant for the penitent alone.
But as soon as you're involved
with this edifice, you come under
her influence: the crooked, creaking,
teetering funhouse feeling of being
in a place just lateral to the norm.
You can expect the lock at the top
of the stairs is not a one-handed
flick-of-the-wrist affair and won't yield
before you've questioned your sanity.
Inside, you'll notice how not even
the faucets can get it together;
how hot and cold are kept apart,

how warmth is not on tap;
how the carcass-shaped rads
coiled under the windows
draw the air through their ribs
with the vapour of all your breath and sweat,
wringing you dry to the particle.

Mommy & Daddy Smoke a Little Weed

Mommy and Daddy smoke a little weed,
burn candles in bottles, don't watch much TV.
I was suckled on wonder, grew up among dreams.

I'm Sepia Boy, the child in old photos
with eyes sunk deep in questioning shadows.
I'm the Beatnik's kid who smells of tobacco.

Mommy calls me Owl for my big round eyes.
Daddy calls stupid what Mommy calls wise.
But nobody's bothered; everyone's high.

Mommy and Daddy are always dead broke.
They'll ask you your sign and offer a toke.
My folks play life by tealeaf and Tarot.

We wander like carnies, live in our ride.
Mommy says Daddy tells too many lies.
But nobody's bothered; everyone's high.

Mommy and Daddy smoke a little weed,
burn candles in bottles, don't watch much TV,
forget where they park, cruise at low speeds.

Sensitive Ears

On the Amtrak from Chicago to Indianapolis, I hear one gaming
behind me and turn to find a zombie: earbuds, thumbs at a laptop.
Twice I request a reduction in volume despite the distance

between us, despite how deep the music is buried in his skull.
Clearly he is half deaf. Nevertheless, he remarks, indignant
and without irony, *Wow! You have sensitive ears.*

Is it because mother is a survivor and father died at fifty-four
the world troubles me? Even in drunken numbness,
the machinery of death whistles at my hackles.

Imagine every hair upon the skin represents a nerve-ending
every hair—even those invisible blond hairs and those preened away
so one might appear more loveable and less sensitive.

Yes. More *sensible*, as the French put it. I am more in the flesh.
And still—among the dreaming, I am taken for a dreamer.

Free Spirit

She called me a free spirit. How rude!
It made me scowl. It made me brood—

entirely ruined the night for me.
I just sat there like an owl up in a tree.

In my mind, I strung it up on its head,
hoisted it up like something dead.

How am I less bound than she?
How is she more bound than me?

I dressed the question like a swine
and peeled back the heavy hide.

(I was free of *her* master, she of mine;
we were free but not untied.)

Alas, those thoughts escaped my mind
that night and the next. Thus years went by.

Often I brooded over that one pique;
it marked my heart with an extra beat.

And when I tried to be, I felt caught
in the act, still apprentice to my part,

while from her karats, she bestowed
that arresting euphemism upon my soul.

Loving Friday

If you spoke to me in your language,
a language I do not understand,
I would watch you as one upon the shore
observes the incomprehensible sea.

And this is as it should be between
you and me: each foreign, each a mystery
no language can spell away, no magic
(not even sex) can penetrate.

Come to think of it, I wish to never
understand the babble of any lover,
for then anger would be but blunt anger
without dangerous, daggerous insult.

Silence is oxygen to affection's flame:
it's quiet warmth and quiet light,
till words flit in like errant moths,
and tiny agonies erupt mid-flight.

Poached Pleasure

Whatever else, there must be pleasure
and best of all, stolen pleasures,
filched like eggs, delicate as eggshells,
delectable and variable of texture,
and of use!—as glue, as glaze, as fluff and foam
—O, pleasures like eggs best stolen:

stolen hours in each other's arms …
quickies; how much sweeter
is time stolen for writing
than the time set aside to write.
Time and eggs and love and sex.

Such delicacy spiced with such depravity,
salted liberally,
buttered …
enjoyed thoroughly.

Stolen pleasures emerge from this yolk
submerged in its whites
with all the potential to feather or fry,
or even spill out a solar system,
swirl out into a milky way.

O, atomic delight!—the bright
centre holds as the transparent blast slipping,
slims out, stretching to its limits …

and my heart full of wishes
eggs it on
        and runs *with* it.

Sweet Little Death

For Amanda

I fashioned a bed of cedar and spruce;
built it high and wide. It is a field of love,
a warren of pleasures.

We make love there, my beloved and I,
and we slumber in each other's arms
without care. At wee hours though

the old bladder stirs, disturbing sleep,
and, heeding nature's call, I descend
the high cloud and shuffle

down the dark hallway to the toilet,
where I relieve myself in darkness,
half dreaming, longing to return

to dreams, to be wrapped again in blankets
with the soporific breath of my beloved
and the musky odour of her sweat.

Returning to bed in darkness,
I smell her there, and it feels like
all the goodness of the earth

I'd known as a child returned to me;
I returned to myself. And I think,
God, I pray death amounts to this:

a slight lift before joining that aroma.
And I draw closer to her, and she,
without waking, nestles closer to me.

Metamorphosis

She misses and dismisses my words, and I fly into rages.
Were I a buffalo and she a lion, the uproar and commotion
would prove no more calamitous.

She pounds at my door, demanding love, igniting passions.
Were we pornstars, we'd put the structures of our furnishings
and the very floorboards to no greater test.

She is possessive, and jealous she cannot know
with any certainty what love, what spite, what betrayal
flits the synapses so unquietly behind my gaze.

I am an explosive device she arms and disarms.
She hopes to detonate me safely in her bombproof embraces,
but the spunk she draws only inflames her jealousy.

O, how she hates it!—that unknowable place within me;
that space I myself barely know. She demands inflorescence.
She will have that protean core if it costs her her sanity.

And indeed it wears on her mind like a massive multiplayer
online roleplaying game she has imagined into existence
from a stray theatre ticket and an unknown caller.

Consequences be damned! She'll snoop, throw open every door
in Bluebeard's home, and upbraid him upon his return.
She calls and I flee fast. She calls and I am wood.

Spilt Milk

I'd counted myself well acquainted with spills;
had absorbed many a splash, many an overturned cup; but this,
this was like twenty years' worth in one shot:

I'd dropped the carton, and half its guts throbbed out
like blood from a spluttering wound.
Never had I spilled so much milk.

Either the occluded circuits of my brain conspired the upset
to deliver an urgent metaphor; or the sheer vastness
of all this intimate substance pooling at my feet

forced a crisis. This was not your proverbial spilt milk.
It demanded a fuss. Misjudging the actual depth
and consistency of the mess, I threw in a good half-metre

of paper-towels. Instantly, they were soaked, dripping
a slippery milky-way to the trash; and soon enough,
the tragedy is wicking through my socks.

So I cast more paper into this luciferous white hole,
then more, and—I hesitate to say—still more—hoping,
I guess (and forgive me), that enough tissue will resolve any issue.

Now I've got a sopping mass of guilt the size of my head
on my hands, for I have been so lawless and wasteful,
no toilet can swallow what I've done.

Plumbing Trouble

The trouble lies behind the drywall
somewhere; I don't know where.
Beyond sight, beyond the reach of my mind,
the pipeline snakes into psychic depths:

coiling round imaginings, clogging the works.
Nothing I do will do until I break through,
cut open that pipe and find the truth.
Beyond a half-inch of drywall lies the future.

There will be dust and debris. No way
to avert upheaval now, not after the cold lye
and the fuming acid and the lithe blind auger
have failed to unclog the matter.

It's time for the drill; it's chisel time;
the sledge hammer must swing. It pains
my ass, but better my ass than my soul.
When finally I lay my eyes and hands

on the culprit, it will quit its mysterious slithering
behind the wall; it will gain substance,
become sensible, yield to reason and a little
elbow grease; and my kitchen sink will gasp;

a whorl will form in the standing water,
and that gorgeous gasp and gurgle of relief
will follow, agreeing with all creation, swilling
its silvery self to a point, twisting to its true depth.

SINKHOLE

Spell of Moths

Moth: Born of dust.
Like dust, move—you must!

Queen of Dust,
dusted in gold—up. Up!

Shiver shimmer by.
Flash a wing upon the eye.

Into the fabric, flit and fly,
spin your spawn and die.

Moth! Sew dust and hide.
Lust in cloth and multiply.

Turtle Beyond Light Speed

Chinless but determined, turtle reaches his destination
to find the world has changed. Not only have the cycling heavens
worn and shed their wools and cottons a few times over,
but the landscape, who hides and who hunts and what leaves
rustle what intricate puzzles over sky and ground,

indeed, all he's learned of the place, all he's come his long way
        seeking
—marvels of his trade to study; masters of his craft with whom
to turtle about the mushroom garden; amphibious women as at
        home
in the mucky riverbed as in the dry bed of the wind—
all of it faded to shades of sepia.

Poor turtle, the land he saw when he was a small faraway gleam
was distant as a star; its light a glow of days gone by.
But the land beyond that light was the future he's entered now
—a shade more wrinkling in the neck; and knocking around in
        his shell,
a green vision that doesn't age but has nonetheless grown old.

Fits & Misfits

There's always an unforeseen factor
that'll melt a nuclear reactor,

but what one fails to imagine,
in his world doesn't happen,

till it does; upon which he observes,
Well, it isn't supposed to occur.

Never put into so many words,
his thoughts are vorpal swords,

fencing in mythical fields of logic
—half nonsense, half verbal magic.

And this delusional vanity,
this childish toying with reality

is all fine with me (I'm a madman
after all); what rattles my can

is how randomly an age splits
its fits from its misfits,

as though a shift in culture
wouldn't upend the nomenclature,

and, a revolution later, the norm
become the madness of the age before.

The Clean Ones

A far deeper madness
attends a life without madness.

I'm perfectly happy with my cup of coffee,
my morbid thoughts, my melancholy.

Pathologies, after all, are modern myths
sprung from suburban analysts.

All imagination lost
when phantasy was tossed,

they look you over …
diagnose their own disorder.

When bourgeois life plateaus,
they find a madman to expose.

Therefore, let me unleash
the slavering dogs of my beliefs

for all suburbia to hear.
Grab a lawn chair. Crack a beer.

I don't give a rat's ass for table tact;
can't hear horseshit spew and not react.

Unlike clean and mannered folk,
I talk at you with a greasy fork.

The clean ones; now, there's a topic:
twenty-twenty but still myopic.

Unlike the clean ones God picked,
I'm not suicidally metempsychotic.

Due to my unscientific inclinations,
I don't seek truth in replication.

The clean ones are the ones who say
my compulsions do not pay.

Their compulsions, on the other hand,
how are they a better brand?

And what does *pay* mean anyway?
Of the clean ones, I say, Let them bray.

Sinkhole

To think it was there all this time
undermining my dreams as I slept.

Contractor, county and parish
had set my home on hollow ground.

I read about the city councillor,
the contracts sealed with spit and graft.

I read about the bankers banking
on books cooked up in crooked labs.

Just a month ago, the insurer sent
a geologist to check on his bet.

A pale sceptic came and with a spike,
he poked the soil, grinned, said nothing more.

I suppose America festers
and I fell through the rotten floor.

* * *

I slipped into an ingrown world,
dripping with itself and reaching

for itself from above and below,
marrying itself into draperies and columns,

at once celebrating and mourning itself
in weeping galleries of stone

sweat out in a clammy fever of self-adoration,
evolved drip
            by drop
               over
                eons

until—its skin stretched too thin
from a hopeless economy of feeding on itself

—it collapsed, snapped open.
Like the eyes of a newborn, like the hood

of a cobra, like a camera-shutter,
it captured me among its shadows.

Don't Look Down

Again the illustrator edits the ground
from under Wile E. Coyote's feet,

and the perhaps too-wily coyote, by the grace
of his maker, hangs suspended

just long enough to suss his plight;
just long enough to take one last, easy

breath; just long enough to amuse
with the unreal magic of his oblivion.

O, Wile E., don't look down! I too
have stood upon that groundless ground.

You *can*. You *can* walk on air.
Show us how it's done Wile E.

Keep your eye on a singular, steady point
in the distance, and though your heart drop,

don't look down.

I Must Go to Them

I am told I must go to them.
So reluctantly, I go.
The animals need my help.
It is my duty.

The way is pleasant
along a soft dirt passage,
not well trodden, but clearly,
—with jungle to the left
and to the right, a hazy
ill-defined uncertainty,
the edge of consciousness,
I suppose—this avenue,
perfectly straight
and without end,
is the civilised path.

It is a bright, beautiful day.
And I am happy to be out
and on my way.

Behind me some hundred yards,
a woman and a little girl
are headed toward
the same noble task as I.

Presently, an animal,
part wolf, part hyena,
torn somehow, with another
creature of its kind, dead
and strapped to it
by a contrivance of its own hide
so they seem as one with two heads,
but with a lost look about
the living head, the other hanging
upside down at its side.

I don't know what I'm seeing.
I struggle to make sense of it.

The lady and the girl take one glance
and turn to walk back
where they came from.
They understand immediately
this vision is not propitious
for their mission of charity.

Puzzled and uncertain,
I do not take the hint.

Instead, I carry on toward a clearing
where I am confronted by a menacing,
wide face, prehistorically huge,

its snout buried
up to its two golden eyes
in the heaped carcass
of some indistinct beast,

its two golden eyes
a fiery amber planted in black,
rough-wrinkled flesh, overgrown
with wiry auburn fur soaked
in the mess of its kill.

It glares at me, but without
pausing at its meal, continues
to snort and gorge itself,
with those eyes fixed on me.

Only then do I feel danger
and think the two behind me
have made the right choice.
So I turn on my heel
and make my way back
without haste, not to incite
those ravenous eyes,
putting them out of my head
as though I've witnessed a crime
of which I must never speak.

Golden Bough

I dropped a stone, but heard no splash.
A dried up well? A secret cache?
I had to know. So I lit a fire,

dropped it down, and there below,
the dark gleamed and stirred within,
and awoke an ancient dream.

I fashioned a rope of roots and stems,
then tied one end to a gnarled oak
and shimmied down.

The light above was like a moon
toward which the room was reaching.
I struck a match and lit a branch:

Three archways raised their brows.
One by one, I stared them down,
but couldn't tell the left from right,

nor which might prove the central hall.
I closed my eyes and turned and turned
till occident and orient were lost.

I stopped, and the lurching arches
swinging round unbalanced me.
The sand underfoot broke my fall.

Thus I sat upon the ground with fire
in my hand and a choice to make.
I reasoned I might as well take the one

before me as who knew but all three
were one, or all amounted to as much,
and onward I tread into the mystery.

The Tale of Trudging Tiberius

I woke up and the world was silent
because the sun was wadded away in cloud,
and the earth was buried under dunes of snow.
I didn't want to get up. There was nowhere to go.

Nevertheless, I did get up and go
out into the dark day into the moonish snow,
into the clobbering cold, into the hushed world to trudge
because that's what you do … though no bear,

as deep as he is stuffed in his fur and fat,
would subject himself to that … that wasteland.
Nope. That's what us humans do, plying intellect.
And what power do you suppose pressed me?

It was duty. And what is duty? I thought,
as I trudged. It's some concoction of fear and love
and courage and pride. Yes, pride, for what
would become of the world if I did not go out

into the godless, dreary day and trudge?
What savage peace, what morbid tranquillity
would reign here if I did not impose my dutiful boots
on the virgin white dust, or split the easy air

with the axehead of my call. And fear too.
Fear's pitchfork pitched me like a hay bale
into that place I did not want to go.
Truth is, I fear the burning eyes of my fellows,

for they are always there like demons,
watching, prodding me with those jealous embers
smouldering in their hungry skulls.
And so it takes courage to endure them.

And love? Perhaps love is neither necessary
to duty nor certain. I trudged and found it nowhere.
So I left the desolate place, left the planet
for the new, smooth moons of Saturn.

But there was nowhere to settle, just endless
trudging, endless prodding eyes haunting
the black skull of space, and cold worse than snow.
At least my fiery fellows had heat.

But when I returned to the Earth, they were no more.
They'd burnt themselves out with their fire,
and scorched all living things. The sun wore a black veil.
The ground was heaped with ash.

All duty burnt away. But still the rest remained,
for I trembled with fear and cried out with pride
against the blazing ruin of my kind and felt
my courage collapse like a dead star.

Only love—that mystery—eluded me still.
Dear Reader (if there are any readers left),
Understand, I was born as my fellows were emptying
the heart like a closet of childhood junk,

and out went the moon itself and the stars
and the flowers and everything we called lovely.
It was all makebelieve to their dead eyes; and I,
I was the last to lodge these forsaken derelicts.

Workflow 2010

As we flow out of the metro, a fluid flush
of hurrying bodies, the sound of worn-down
rubber soles sweeping along smooth stone
is a sad, domesticated shuffle of creatures

conditioned by the sting of electric fence-wire;
nothing like the long, quickening, knot-releasing rush
of rain or waterfall, nothing like the many-uncrinkling currents
of a river boondoggling around jagged rocks, purling

digressions in eddies off to the side among floating sticks,
fallen leaves and rafts of torn up grasses, gathering itself
with foaming determination to rush over the shoals
of a narrowing shallow—these current-forces pounding

perilously against the pressures of the air as if
they could overtake their banks, leap defiantly
from the gravitational drag and claim the atmosphere
are nothing like the sound of our movements:

of nylon sleeves and nylon legs scraping by
with a grave, hollow sound, and salt-worn shoes
shifting upon a fine dusting of bitter salt and gritty mud;
aggressive bulls pulling fast manoeuvres to circumvent the lame,

snorting behind the slow, bolting at their chance.
With what drive the hobbled struggle in the flow
over the steep stony stairways to make it through the stiles
turning us out, tagged, branded, nose to the digits.

Zombie Domestic

When Stella came home that afternoon,
she was hunched, downcast, electrostatic
as though she'd lost some precious item,
was now upset with herself, retracing steps.

Whatever it was, she couldn't figure it.
Her husband embraced her. *There there*, he said,
there there. But Stella was not there or here.
She grunted, knit her brow and gaped at him.

They took dinner with Netflix, estranged,
as if ten years of prison had kept them apart,
but no such excuse. An odour lingered in her wake.
Cushions required frequent airing.

The bite took time, but one day, Mr Stella sniffed,
and behold, the rancid smell had departed!
In fact, his olfactory nerve had withered. No matter,
he was more content without the sense.

ZOMBIE APOCALYPSE

Diagnosis

The illness spread with especial ease
because so many bore no symptoms.
To most, it wasn't a sickness at all,
just another benign virus in the system.

Hatched by the doctors of safety,
the methods to prevent worst fears,
intensified our basest inclinations
to exist in electronic spheres.

Life to us was something planned.
Insurers, those bookies of the unforeseen,
with transubstantiative maths,
exchanged dollars for adversities.

This way, we cushioned loss,
cheated death itself by windfalls.
In time, we couldn't face any real danger;
we simply lacked the wherewithal.

A metaphysic of the ledger ruled,
stealing quality from life in measures,
till joy and passion gave us the slip,
for all we knew were calculated pleasures.

At last, we preset all machinery to defaults
to enable thoughtless zombiekind,
that it might move about as shadows
of a world the living left behind.

The Zombie Train

The zombies have tread endless miles through time.
Baron Samedi, in tails, digs love a fresh grave.
They've stolen through ages eating life out of mind.

They've shuffled in file to the Baron's high style,
his top hat in hand, his cigar, his rum and his cane.
The zombies have tread endless miles through time.

They usher death into fashion, use trends as their blind.
Now it's high boots; now Jews, now the unvaxxed are to blame.
They've stolen through ages eating life out of mind.

Since the great armies of Cyrus drank rivers dry,
historical crossings have graven terrible names.
The zombies have tread endless miles through time.

The cause is convincing when God's on your side.
The cause is their Voodoo. The cause makes it plain.
They've stolen through ages eating life out of mind.

Baron Samedi is ugly, but he's dressed to the nines:
he staggers in pinstripe, bloodshot eyes behind shades.
The zombies have tread endless miles through time.
They've stolen through ages eating life out of mind.

I Am Maledictus

Ma was a virgin of a humble home.
Da was a righteous, holy soul.
They dragged me screaming from my hole.

Out of the sweet womb I ran mad.
Such a scowl greeted me, I stabbed
and gouged its foul eyes with my bare hands.

I am the one who was there by the tree.
I chose the apple. I sewed the seed.
I am the one who set man free.

I squirm through all hearts equally.
Who lies to himself provokes me
to set his mind acrawl with unrealities.

Who fails to see, I blind literally.
Who will not open, I shut in misery.
Who ignores me, festers in his piety.

I pave the dirty road of matrimony.
I am the pleasures of sex. I am ecstasy.
I wade the energy, ripple the frequency.

I marked Cain for self-reflection.
I made the rain that drowned creation.
Mine is the tongue in the ear of the virgin.

Mine is the odour of manure.
I am the callous of the calmly inured.
While Gilgamesh slept, I swallowed the cure.

I put the coal in the hand of the child.
I sprung the vine that juices the wild.
Mine is the twist of the final smile.

I instructed Hammurabi, Plato and Marx.
I set mountain folk upon valley folk just for a lark.
I've led tribal minions into the dark.

I informed Moses, Cyrus and Caesar,
stood with Calvin, Robespierre and Hitler.
I'll rent righteousness to any believer.

I shared with Goya the Quinta del Sordo.
I stoked the Maenads when Orpheus moaned.
I usher the frenzy of death from the shadows.

Call me, Maledictus, Master of Curses.
I worm into your inward most searches.
I muster the justice that's made into verses.

iTard

With a ghoulish glow upon his face,
he sifts through the data junkyard,
through the electronic gossip, gossip, gossip,
through the science and the stats,
the stats, the stats, palming the questions
that invent the stats, with a cross-eyed cue
for you too to set yourself askew:
what % are you? He sifts through this,
this, this, what is it? He'll set it aside
for later review. Is this what we'll do?
Is this from now on what it all amounts to?
Is this the material truth?—mental mixology?
brain chemistry? the marketing view?
Combing the net, the catch is redundant
in both the bountiful sense and in the sense
of being all but repugnant. What context
can corral the data?—cull the trivial,
white noise raging through the feeds,
feeding the chemical children false food,
setting up psychic switches and triggers
that can be flicked, pulled, fired like bolts?
With a ghoulish glow upon his face,
he sifts through gossip and stats,
through this and that, bits and scraps,
now angry, now appalled, now laughing
an unsettling, otherworldly laugh,
as upon the neuronal shift and sway

over a sea of symbols, a shaky language,
hovering like a fog, shrouds the soul
in a pod of wispy screens and soft logic.

Zombie Apocalypse

After Solzhenitsyn

It wasn't the way the fictional accounts had proposed. It seldom is.
They weren't bloody and ugly at all. No torn limbs,
no eyes rolled back, no menacing arms or grabby hands.

They weren't especially pretty, mind you.
There was a surge in the plastic surgery practice
as well as in the cosmetics trade. Perfume too,

to cover that smell. That smell was new:
a mild odour of three-day old fish, a whiff of cheese
escaping its wraps, something to raise the old whiskers.

But it was all so subtle, we could make excuses;
sometimes we had to: who would be the paranoiac
to raise the alarm about the *Stinky Food Craze?*

Prices went through the roof. Cheese makers
became cheese magnates, durian growers, durian barons.
Turned out later, they weren't eating any of it.

They were buying it to excuse that smell.
It was like that. There were minuscule social changes
you could observe on the roads and sidewalks,

and in the subways: less general alertness,
a peripheral blindness hard to catch among so many
zoned out, headphoned and focused on their own hands.

But a mysteriously dull mood gradually crept over life.
Alcohol consumption rose, while the prophylactics market
suffered in proportion to the upswing in cosmetics.

It's not that folk were having more unprotected sex:
birthrates plummeted. Everywhere you turned your head,
it seemed love was staggering away on its last legs.

* * *

With uncharacteristic initiative and in a baffling display
of energy, the zombies designed forms for every action imaginable:
for raising an arm, for lifting a finger, batting an eye, bending a leg.

They struck endless committees and review panels to deliberate
form reform and how to put one foot in front of another,
with special amendments granting special provisions,

not *privileges*, mind you, but *provisions*: social aid
for those requiring nose jobs, tummy tucks, reconstruction.
Folks had to fit in after all. There was great concern over *adjustment*.

Refusal to fill out a form became punishable under the Treason Act.
Everyone at some point forgot a form, there were so many.
But that was the game. It accounted for the disappearances.

And wow, were the regulations ever a fine filigree!
Such intricacies suggested architecture, but in truth it was proof
against intelligent design to behold such a collusion of accidents.

The Ghoul Guard

Some, no matter how much you bit them,
could not be turned. *Difficult to get along with,*
we'd call them, but they didn't care.

We'd shout them down, wag our heads,
frown them into submission. *You couldn't leave it be,*
we'd say, then turning our backs, we'd shun them.

Since sanity is but a matter of consensus,
we made them feel insane by our numbers,
by drumming into them the true complexities.

But there's a type that just won't heed,
a sort that can't help but buck authority, that snaps
the chain in the teeth of the winch.

To each his time of death and pain,
but God made some for boot and club,
and the rest He made for powder and slug.

Soul Resistant Material

We have educated ourselves out of a soul, gone
into the world, grabbed every grouse of a thing,
and following a few clinical incisions, stepped
on its feet and skinned the beauty clean off.

We've engineered soul proof matter: psychically
resistant up to several fathoms, dream-repellent
and magic-deflectant. Coated with a love-hindering
polymer, it requires zero maintenance.

One enters certain establishments and senses
a vibeless indifference. It's tied to the generic,
mass produced sheen, the lack of personality,
the feeling you might as well be almost anywhere.

Every new bar in my neighbourhood is a variation
of the same algorithm, cut from the same matrix.
Observing certain sexy citizens in this new market,
I am aroused by their plastic-cast, calisthenicsised

curves, calculated down to the very lips. Their mass
produced pants feel wirelessly linked to my own.
Admittedly, their perfume broadcasts desire effectively
as a cat trailed by a string of toms. Apocalypse

never smelled so good. Noting those whose hair
resembles in both colour and texture the brushed steel
gleaming in every renovated kitchen in the West,
I feel those cuts preliminary to flaying. Once the skin

is peeled off, how does one embrace? Paint raw flesh
with smart hide. Let the network learn to distinguish
your screams: which from ecstasy, which from pain.
Let lover from assailant be, like meat from bone, reclaimed.

Zombie Genius

After Thucydides

Enough were esteemed geniuses, no word remained
to name one so skilled he could hold forth upon all domains,
and tangled confusions thrashed in the airwaves
as ordinary stones were sold for crystals in spades.

Nevertheless, many did spew smart drivel
and what passed for clever was to level your whistle
at a frequency audible only to fools and devils,
a signal that snake oil was passing for elixir.

Knowing they themselves were slow, they set up a show
of baffling equations to deflect the natural flow
of inquiry and delay the progress of faster fellows.
For generations, many hung their heads and held their noses.

While the quick were busy unravelling boondoggle,
the slow but clever were floating in pools, necking bottles.
You see, the slow ones weren't as dim as their goggles;
they knew their lies would soon be unknotted.

They also knew the invaders were near.
So they made arrangements well ahead of their peers
who were too prudent for action, too caught up in the gears
of the state apparatus and their retirement years.

In the end, I suppose one couldn't distinguish
zombie from genius. They both lumbered and languished,
let the heart ground dry, let dreams waste famished.
Genius had sold its brand, and in a blink it was bankrupt.

Four Quartets for Zombies

1.
Picture T.S. Eliot as Magus, stopping a rain drop mid-air,
asking of it how it turns the world on its head, inquiring
whence it came, what relation to the fountain
into which it will shortly merge and ping concentric rings.

Hard to imagine Thomas Stearns dancing, letting loose.
Pedantic fallacies aside, we suspect he is Prufrock,
afraid of peaches, their suggestive juice upon his chin.
(O, humour so highfalutin, who laughs among the bushes?)

But here's Tom Magus dancing between rain drops,
between past and present, afraid of getting wet.
He has good reason, because Tom, you see, would like to be
a Tesla of poetry, one who grounds electricity.

A cloud full of lightning settles over his laboratory.
Upon his counter, a compass, a crucified frog, notes.
At heart, it's a romantic experiment, but the air
is so thick with erudition, he floats above the earth.

Let us go now where Tom cavorts with mermaids
and drown him in human voices in the fountain
in dangerous weather under the cloud under the roses
where the present dies and the past lies etherized.

2.

Hard to imagine Thomas Stearns at sex, but picture
him nevertheless—an anatomically intact Ken doll,
engaging that end of life, taking the creative force
by the hips, as it were; knocking at heaven's door.

One wonders, did he ever make it? Come. Let us
make our terrestrial visit. Dog, dig love up again
where it gangrenes in the chest of that corpse
in the unreal city. Pinch your nose, roll up your sleeves.

Breathe.

You stir stagnant waters. (Do not ask, *What dream is this?*)
Remember her hair catching sun, a solar flare,
as kingfishers catch fire, as lenses reflect, pupils glare;
and so she sits at the bottom of the stair,

shielding such wonderful eyes as awaken eyes everywhere.
Weave sunlight and hair. We are almost there.
Spells last a spell only and new poets plough hell,
drop seed, speak sparks and drive the black mares;

hooves flashing, cleave dark, the sheen of their coats
rivering, rushing their gleam over the beams of the moon,
pressing through shrouds of gloom. Look there again,
and see again: witness the heart in its grim cage sing.

And when the heart dies, with his words, he digs it up again,
defibrillates, syncopates, hops between drops—at least
Hopkins does, and Thomas in his wake, like Reggae sprung
on frogs' legs leaping green from stagnant waters.

3.
In the good old days, Tom Magus needed merely turn a phrase,
and the rain drop obeyed. Now the great globe itself
is a substantial, overcrowded pageant, and the rain crashes
upon an ordinary man, soaking him, tearing through roses,

driving the laughter out of the bushes shrieking
into the shape of children. The once ecstatic act turned
spectator-sport, turned porn, and no trick up any sleeve
escapes the singular gravity of innuendo.

So the wet hierophant must screw deeper into prose,
exchange his starry robes for a trench coat, a cape,
a reversible poncho, that he might turn the outside in
and the inside out before diving after himself.

Trouble is, when Thomas Stearns gazes into the mirror,
a wintery erudition sweeps in, crystalizing his reflection.
Too much reality, sore footed, refractory, world-wizened,
we plod a burnt wasteland with parched camel.

The mind coils under a rock of the brain to hide from magi
who sling slogan and symbol like a bolas, tripping me into you,
spell-binding first person I after I into fasces.
Shadows cast the matter and so they see no shadow.

4.
Time present and DJ Boxer finds his grooves, drops
his needles, mixes a medley of time past, and raps
a pastiche-fusion of poetry, spins new unions,
into a clockwise spell turning on borrowed magic.

Not for my ego alone, I pick like a baglady, like Suzanne
in rags and feathers, like a seagull among wasteful tourists
salvaging morsels. By no machinish trick, I must redeem
the shells of the small present for living sand dollars.

One might rightly ask: *Faced with Prufrock's patient*
bled out by barber science—its brain set upon the scale,
its clockwork ticker laid aside—does one turn back with Eliot
to Christ sprawled and wriggling on his pins?

By way of answer, let's revisit Doctor Tom in his lab.
We find he has harnessed reason to voltaic chemistry
and behold as he declares in his best German,

> *It's ALIVE!*

The trouble now is Death himself has risen,

and with what dread teeth, he spreads the poison.
Death in a lab coat mixes up the medicine: and gone
is the fountain, the laughter in the rose bushes;
only accident now ripples air and puddle in the garden.

Zombie Tom laughs at Evil: *Silly superstition, that.*
He seeks instead to explain the cathedral by the quartz
and rust in its rocks; his work confirmed by rounds
of priests who walk the briar, loosing the gowns of desire.

Shrouded in clouds of cordite and mustard gas,
scented with a whiff of Zyklon and Nazi oven-smoke,
with sour notes of death from Vozrozhdeniya, an aftertaste
of rip-roaring rape, of a shadow burnt into a wall;

evil stands defrocked. No poetry can salvage, no aesthetic
rehabilitate, no religion exonerate God. Only atoms now
and molecules remain. Surveillance and chemical castration
will correct the criminal vein of evolution.

Lend the zombie a hand. What harm now? Liberty too
is but a baseless by-product. And love making
and beauty are for dupes who think they have a soul,
fools who seek a wizard at the levers of the world.

Sadly, my friends, the etherized patient has died.
What catalyst, then, turns Thomas Stearns from his lab
toward the mannequins in the sanctuary?

A recognition.
                    Remember that frog on the cross?

When the leg of that frog twitches, the needle
of the compass spins as if bewitched. Magic is alive;
God is afoot. But not as before. This time, magus
and priest wear white coats. They clock, weigh,

measure, tabulate data. Magic, in sober spectacles,
after a deep breath and a coffee break, admits
to simple magnetism, and God rubs his eyes, consults
his watch, says, *This is not what I meant at all.*

The terms have changed and like snakeskin lie in a heap.
That corpse, the mannequins, the cathedral itself
are empty, true. Now, time present, is the time to imbue.
Magic now plays with magnets; God speaks evolution.

The compass points where the twins reflect, where
shadows spring from the lantern, where sparks fork
forth from the dark, volts vault and shock from the naught.
Mannequins do not ignite crusades; zombies, however,

those with pumps for hearts and algorithmic brains,
who heap the world with beans for counting, shadows
who scoff at their own mystery will one night find the world
knows only shadow and amounts to much the same

as when witches brewed, and vampire kings arose,
and mythic knights slew dragons for their gold.
In short, they'll find all the work of ages undone,
for the soul is no vestigial set of gills causing hiccups.

When Thomas Stearns enters the sanctuary, it is not
a turning away, but rather a cabling of the dry, linear mind
to the etheric fountain of phantasy. He braves the Choir,
Sweeney Among the Pederasts, to kick up the old dance.

DJ Boxer plays the flipside in counter-time. Reality emerges
like children with arms spread walking the fountain ledge
—a teetering precessional dance tilting, leaping, laughing,
troubling the rose bushes and the gorgeous world into being.

Acknowledgements

I am lucky to have enjoyed the encouragement of some genuine hearts and generous souls. My mother, Sarah, always proud, even of the worst of it, helped me through the worst of it. A thank you as well to Elisa, my adored sweetheart, for her enduring love. Michael Harris's tacit nod or grunt were like pillars of fire and smoke to this book. And dinners at the Harrises, legendary and rejuvenating, were often enough the bread and wine of inspiration. Thank you to Daniel Bratton and Carol Williams at the Beaver House Poetry Centre in Elora, Ontario for friendship and unforgettable meals, for taking an interest in this work and for going so far as to produce a chapbook of the zombie sequence (*Field Notes for the Undead*). And thank you to Peter Skoggard for setting my poems to music and for making a big deal of my work and for facilitating exciting collaborations. Little has been more rewarding than these collaborations. Thank you to Marko Sijan for a friendship that enjoys all the virtues. And thank you to Marc di Saverio for standing by me with fierce determination. Some of these poems go back far enough I feel I ought to thank Simon Dardick at Vehicule Press for always being friendly and supportive. Thank you, David Solway and Eric Ormsby. Thank you all at Guernica Press: Michael, I must thank for his patience and editorial insight. I'd like to take this opportunity to thank Miranda Hickman for her interest in both my writing and my poetry competition. Without her introductions and interventions and monumental efforts, McGill's English Department would not presently be running *The Montreal International Poetry Prize*, a remarkable marriage. And not even her efforts, it seems, would have sufficed without Richard Pound's invaluable help. As for the rest of you wonderful folk who have stood by me, I will cast a thank-you blanket upon you and remark once more how lucky I am to be surrounded by compassionate individuals. You are a draft of fresh aether that has kept me laughing and loving.

About the Author

Asa Boxer's debut book, *The Mechanical Bird* (2007), won the Canadian Authors Association Prize for Poetry, and his cycle of poems entitled "The Workshop" won first prize in the 2004 CBC Literary Awards. His poems and essays have since been anthologised in various collections and have appeared in magazines internationally. His books include *Skullduggery* (Signal, 2011), *Friar Biard's Primer to the New World* (Frog Hollow Press, 2013), *Etymologies* (Anstruther Press, 2016) and *Field Notes from the Undead* (Interludes Press, 2018). Boxer is also a founder of *The Montreal International Poetry Prize*. He presently edits *The Secular Heretic*, an online magazine for the arts and sciences. And he appears in a weekly cultural video series called *Daymakers* (with fellow writers Marko Sijan and Marc di Saverio) in which he reads poems, conducts interviews with provocative thinkers and participates in conversations on the arts and sciences.

Printed in December 2021
by Gauvin Press,
Gatineau, Québec